THE MAYA

by Judith Lechner

Table of Contents

Introduction

If you travel to a part of Mexico, you will be in for a great surprise. Huge temple ruins and **pyramids** reach high above the jungle trees. A thousand years ago, priests dressed in feather costumes marched up the steps of those pyramids. Musicians beat drums and tooted horns as they followed. Then came the rich men. They wore jewelry made of a beautiful, green stone called jade. The men carried gifts to their gods.

These are the ▶ ruins of a Maya pyramid and temple.

Who were those people? They were the Maya (MAH-yuh). They lived in an area known as Middle America starting around 1000 B.C. The great Maya **civilization** lasted about 1,200 years. The Maya built cities and huge buildings such as temples and palaces. They farmed, played games, and created a written language. They studied the stars and planets.

How did the Maya civilization start? Why did it disappear? What was life like for the Maya? Read this book and find out.

▲ the ruins of Tikal

The Early Days of the Maya

1000 B.C.—A.D. 300

In the early days, the Maya lived in farming villages. They grew corn, beans, squash, chili peppers, and cotton. Men and boys hunted and fished. They raised turkeys for meat and bees for honey. Women and girls wove beautiful cloth. They made pottery with painted flowers and animals on it. There were no kings or chiefs. Maya men took turns as village leaders.

About 600 B.C., things began to change. A rich ruling class emerged. Over several hundred years, these **nobles** built great cities where they lived as rulers and priests. The rest of the people who were farmers lived in small villages nearby.

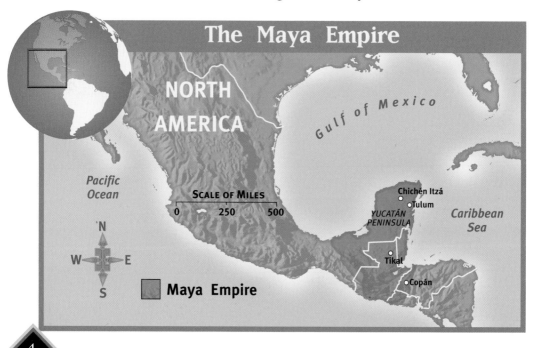

The Maya Empire

NORTH AMERICA

Gulf of Mexico

Pacific Ocean

SCALE OF MILES

0   250   500

N
W—E
S

Chichén Itzá
Tulum
YUCATÁN PENINSULA

Caribbean Sea

Tikal

Copán

Maya Empire

The First Maya Cities

The first Maya cities had pyramids with temples on top. There were also palaces with many rooms for the king, nobles, and priests to live in.

They Made a Difference

The Maya people did not have animals trained to carry loads. They did not have carts with wheels. They did not even have metal tools. Yet they were able to build huge pyramids made of stone blocks. They cut the stone with axes.

▼ **Maya ruins at Palenque**

The cities were the busy centers of Maya life. In the spaces between the temples and palaces, there were large open **plazas** (PLAZ-uhz). Ordinary people gathered in the plazas. They bought and sold goods in crowded markets. People also went to ball courts to watch games played with a large rubber ball.

▲ the Great Plaza at Tikal

The Great Maya Civilization

A.D. 250–925

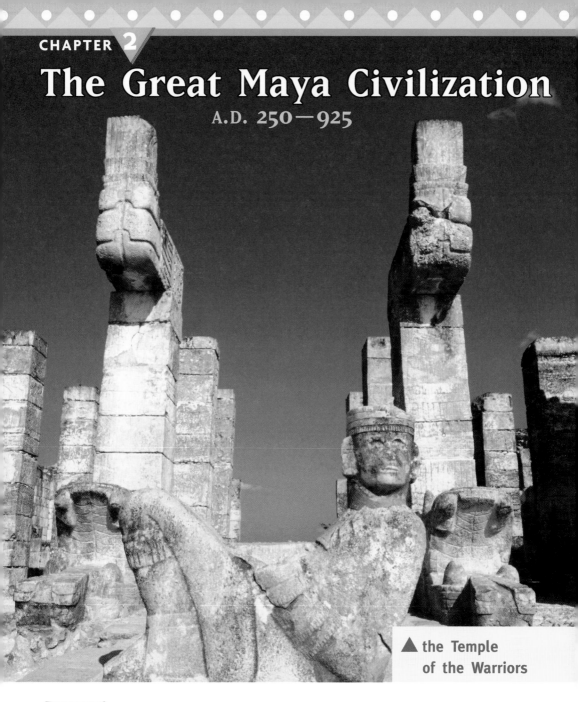

▲ the Temple
of the Warriors

The Maya civilization was at its peak from about A.D. 250 to 925. During that time, the greatest Maya cities were built. About 60,000 people lived in the city of Tikal in A.D. 600. Another 30,000 people lived in the area around the city.

A king ruled Tikal. Most of the kings of Tikal came from one powerful family. There were twenty-nine kings from this family.

Each Maya city was like a separate country. Each city had a king and a government run by nobles. Sometimes, a city joined with another city. They cooperated, or worked together. However, sometimes the cities fought wars against each other. They fought to gain land and to rule more people.

▲ Maya fresco of a battle

Great Pyramids Throughout History

The Maya were not the only people to build pyramids. Ancient Egyptians built pyramids. So did the Aztec of Mexico. Even today, people use the pyramid shape for some buildings.

The Transamerica Pyramid in San Francisco, California, is a modern office building. The builders chose the pyramid shape to make the building safer in an earthquake.

	WHAT	WHERE	WHEN BUILT	HOW TALL
MAYA PYRAMID	Temple of the Two-Headed Snake	Tikal, Guatemala	about A.D. 700	about 210 feet (65 meters)
EGYPTIAN PYRAMID	Great Pyramid of King Khufu	Giza, Egypt	about 2500 B.C.	about 450 feet (137 meters)
MODERN PYRAMID	Transamerica Pyramid	San Francisco, California	A.D. 1970	853 feet (260 meters)

1. SOLVE THIS

a. Which pyramid is the oldest?

b. Which pyramid is the tallest?

c. What is the difference in height between the Maya pyramid and the tallest pyramid?

9

▲ King Pacal's tomb

IT'S A FACT

The Maya believed that their gods needed blood to stay strong. The Maya sacrificed animals to the gods in religious ceremonies. Sometimes the Maya killed people to offer as gifts to the gods.

Maya Religion

The Maya believed that their king was related to the gods. They believed that the king would become a god when he died. But while the king was alive, he had to fight other cities for land, captives, and power. The Maya thought that a victory in war meant the gods liked their king.

Maya kings were buried under the temples of the pyramids. The kings were dressed in their finest clothes and jewels. They were surrounded by goods that they would need in the next world. Servants were sometimes killed and buried with them. The Maya believed that the kings needed the servants in life after death.

Gods and Goddesses

The Maya worshiped many gods and goddesses. The corn god was important to them because corn was their main crop. They prayed to the rain god for rain for their crops. They prayed to the goddess of the moon. She also was goddess of weaving.

The Maya held many religious festivals. People filled the plazas near the temples. They dressed in fancy costumes. Some sang and danced. Musicians played. Clowns and actors wearing masks entertained the people. Storytellers told legends of great kings and heroes.

Maya rain god ▶

Ball Games

The Maya played a ball game called pok-ta-pok (POHK-tuh-POHK). It was like soccer. Boys and men played this game for fun. But it also had another purpose.

Pok-ta-pok was played at religious festivals. The games were held on decorated stone courts in the city. Two teams of players hit a large rubber ball around the court. The players could not touch the ball with their hands or feet. They could only use their arms, hips, thighs, chests, and heads.

▲ Maya ball court

Historical Perspective

Almost every Maya city had its own ball court. Ball games were an important part of Maya life. They were also an important part of Maya religion. Today ball games are still part of everyday life. Most cities and towns have at least one ball field. But our games are just games. They have no connection to religion.

The players were usually young noblemen. They wore padding on their chest, hips, back, and knees. They also wore long deerskin pants. The pants protected the players when they had to dive down on the stone floor of the court.

The rubber ball was made from the sap of a tree. It weighed about five or six pounds. It may have been the world's first rubber ball.

◀ This stone carving shows a player about to hit a rubber ball.

13

Everyday Life of Maya People

Imagine that you are a Maya boy or girl. You are going on a shopping trip to the market. You have a few cocoa beans to use as money to buy a treat for yourself. The day is bright and sunny. The market is packed with people. You go from stall to stall. What beautiful things there are for sale!

You do not have enough money for an animal skin or jewelry. You walk past the bird sellers and wish for a parrot as a pet. Even a clay whistle shaped like a bird costs too much. The only thing you can buy is a food treat. Most people are selling vegetables and fruits. One woman is selling honey. You pay her with a cocoa bean and take your treat home.

Where did all the goods in the market come from? Maya farmers grew vegetables. They raised turkeys and doves for meat, and bees for honey. The Maya hunted deer and wild pig-like animals.

Hunters used blowpipes to shoot birds for their feathers. People who lived near the ocean brought shellfish, salt, shells, and pearls to the markets.

✔ POINT

Picture It

Picture yourself visiting a Maya city. Draw a picture postcard showing what you saw. Then write a message to a friend telling about your visit.

◀ Maya society

Maya Farmers

Maya farmers had different ways of farming different kinds of land. In the highlands, they had good, thick soil and enough rain. Farmers there used wooden digging sticks and hoes with stone blades to plant crops.

In the rain forest, Maya farmers used a method called "slash and burn." They cut down trees in the fall. They burned the trees in the winter. The burned wood made the thin soil richer and better for growing things.

In the wet lowlands, farmers dug canals. The canals drained water from the land. Farmers piled up the earth from the canals to make raised fields for farming.

Maya Canals

NASA scientists took this photograph from space. It shows the canals the Maya built hundreds of years before.

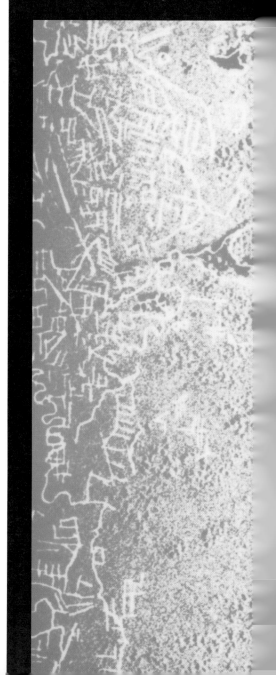

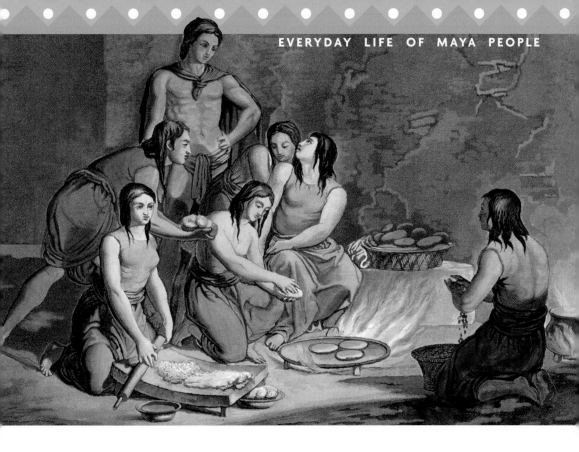

Maya Families

Maya farm families were often large. Grandparents, parents, and children lived together in several small houses. The houses were set around an open area. Houses were made of stone, mud bricks, or wooden poles covered with dried mud. The roofs were made of palm leaves. Each house had only two rooms.

Nobles and Others

The nobles lived a very different life. Their homes were large houses or palaces in the cities. Nobles ran the government. Some were priests of the Maya religion. They wore fine clothing decorated with bright feathers and bits of jade. They wore fancy headdresses to show their high rank.

There was also an "in-between" class of people. They were people who did skilled jobs. Some made pottery or jewelry, or wove cloth. Others were artists and entertainers. Others worked for the government, or were soldiers.

Maya nobleman

peasant woman weaving cotton cloth

Maya Achievements

The Maya had a system of writing. They recorded, or wrote down, their history. They had a system of numbers and math, which they used in their building projects. They observed the stars and planets and made a calendar.

Writing

Maya writing looks like a set of pictures. Each "picture" is called a **glyph** (GLIF). Each glyph stands for a word or the name of a person, place, or event.

They Made a Difference

An Englishman named Sir Eric Thompson (1898–1975) spent fifty years studying Maya writing. He made a list of all Maya glyphs. Many experts studied this list. Thompson's work helped them find out the meanings of most of the glyphs.

Maya glyphs were carved ▶ in stone.

Maya glyphs were carved on stone buildings and on tall stone pillars. These glyphs told of the deeds of kings and gods. Glyphs were also painted on walls inside palaces and temples. Glyphs were painted on pottery that people used every day.

The Maya had books made of bark paper. These books recorded their history, religion, and science. Only specially trained people called **scribes** could read and write. The scribes wrote everything by hand. They were important people who worked for the kings and priests.

IT'S A FACT

Maya books could tell us about Maya life. Sadly, only a few books are left. When the Spaniards arrived, they burned the Maya books. The Spaniards of the 1500s believed the books were "works of the devil." Now scientists have only the stone carvings and paintings of Maya glyphs to study.

Number System

The Maya wrote numbers using dots and bars. Each dot stands for 1. Each bar stands for 5. The number of dots and bars tells what the number is.

2. SOLVE THIS

Study the Maya number system. Use the dots and bars to write the answers to the following questions and problems.

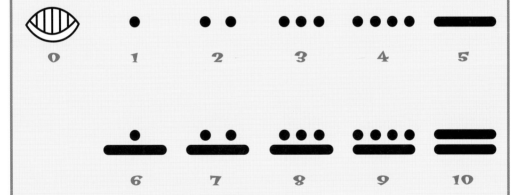

a. How many hands do you have?
b. How many fingers do you have?
c. How many eggs are in a half dozen?
d. What is 12 − 4?

Astronomy

The Maya priests were also scientists. They studied the stars and planets. They watched the movements of the sun and the phases in the moon. They used this information to create a calendar.

The Maya calendar had 365 days like our own. It was divided into 18 months of 20 days each. There were five days left over. Those days were thought to be very unlucky. The Maya stopped eating and made sacrifices to their gods during the "unlucky" time.

The Maya made charts that showed the movements of the stars and planets. The charts were very good. This is amazing because they had no telescopes.

3. SOLVE THIS

The Maya had special names for groups of years.
1 year = 1 tun
20 years = 1 katun
400 years = 1 baktun

How many years are in 5 baktuns and 13 katuns?

◀ Maya
observatory

Arts and Crafts

Archaeologists (ar-kee-AHL-uh-jihsts) are people who study the past. They dig up ruins (ROO-inz) to find ancient objects and buildings from long ago. In one Maya city, the archaeologists found an ancient temple. Three rooms of the temple were decorated with colorful wall paintings. These paintings are called **murals** (MYOOR-uhlz). The murals showed people at festivals. Some pictures were of warriors in battles. The murals were probably painted around A.D. 800.

Archaeologists also have found pottery. Pictures of gods, rulers, and ballplayers were painted on the pottery. The painters used bright red, yellow, blue, and brown paints.

▼ This mural shows Maya warriors.

Jade jewelry was a favorite of Maya nobles. The king and other nobles wore jade necklaces, earrings, and bracelets. They wore bands of jade above their ankles and wide belts around their hips. Their cotton and deerskin clothes were decorated with bits of jade.

▲ Jade was found in riverbeds. This hard green stone was made into beautiful jewelry.

▲ Pacu (PAH-koo), a king, was buried with a jade mask over his face.

IT'S A FACT

Some Maya nobles even wore jade in their teeth. They had holes drilled in their teeth and filled them with jade. They did this for decoration.

▲ This painted vase shows ballplayers in a game.

CHAPTER 5

Later Times of the Maya

A.D. 900–1500s

Beginning about A.D. 900, the Maya left their cities in the lowlands of Guatemala. No one knows exactly why this happened. But archaeologists make some guesses. They think that there was a time of very little rain. The farmers could not feed the city people, and the city people left. Or perhaps the peasants rose up against the rich nobles and drove them away.

The Maya civilization began to move to new places. New cities were built in the Yucatán Peninsula in Mexico and the highlands of Guatemala. Chichén Itzá (CHEE-chen EET-zuh) became the most powerful of all Maya cities.

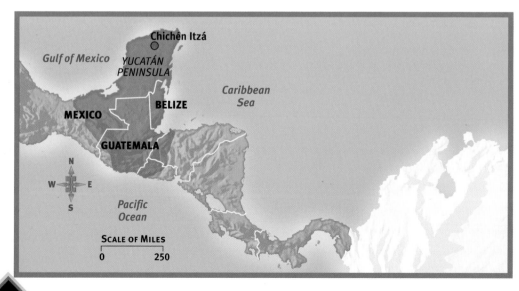

The Spanish Conquest

There were still Maya cities when the Spaniards arrived in A.D. 1528. The Spanish **conquerors** (KONG-kur-urz) were amazed by the Maya cities. But they thought the Maya religion was evil. The Spaniards destroyed Maya temples and statues of the gods. Other Spanish settlers came to live in the Maya land. The Maya cities fell into ruin and were forgotten. Most Maya worked for the Spaniards on farms or as servants.

El Castillo ▶ Pyramid at Chichén Itzá in Mexico

✓ POINT

Talk About It

What made the Maya civilization great? Talk about Maya achievements with other students.

Conclusion

The Maya cities were forgotten for hundreds of years. Then, in 1839, two men found the ruins of a Maya city in the jungle.

What was the Maya civilization like? What happened to this civilization? Use the time line to help answer the questions.

▲ This stone head in Guatemala is more than 1,400 years old.

Time line of the Maya People

1000 B.C.	600–300 B.C.	400 B.C.–A.D. 250	A.D. 250–925
Maya settle in what is now Guatemala.	Maya begin to build cities.	Maya writing, number system, and calendar are used in many Maya cities.	Maya civilization reaches its height. Kings rule great cities.

▲ 19th-century drawing of a Maya pyramid

A.D. 900–1000	A.D. 1528	A.D. 1839	Present
Many Maya cities are abandoned.	Spaniards conquer the Maya.	Two men find the ruins of a Maya city in the jungle.	Maya people still live in Guatemala and Mexico.

In this book, you read about how the Maya civilization began. You visited great Maya cities. You saw how the Maya people lived. You learned that the great Maya civilization disappeared. But the Maya did not die out completely. There are Maya today who continue many customs that began long ago.

▲ Maya women weave cloth the same way they have for centuries.

Glossary

archaeologist   (ahr-kee-AHL-uh-jist) a person who studies the remains of things and people from long ago (page 24)

civilization   (sihv-uh-lih-ZAY-shuhn) the way of life of a people (page 3)

conqueror   (KONG-kur-ur) someone who takes control of a group of people through war (page 27)

glyph   (GLIF) a picture or symbol that stands for a word (page 19)

mural   (MYOOR-uhl) a painting made on a wall (page 24)

noble   (NOH-buhl) a person of the highest social class (page 4)

plaza   (PLAZ-uh) an open public space where people meet and activities take place (page 6)

pyramid   (PIHR-uh-mihd) a building that has a square base and four triangular sides that meet at a point on top (page 2)

scribe   (SKRIBE) a person who copies books and other writings by hand (page 20)

Index

SOLVE THIS ANSWERS

1. Page 9
   a. The Egyptian Pyramid
   b. The Transamerica Pyramid
   c. The difference in height is 643 feet (195 meters).

2. Page 21 a. . . b. ══
   c. ·— d. ···

3. Page 22 2,260 years